Original title:
Life in the Lichen

Copyright © 2025 Creative Arts Management OÜ
All rights reserved.

Author: Olivia Sterling
ISBN HARDBACK: 978-1-80567-273-9
ISBN PAPERBACK: 978-1-80567-572-3

Chronicles of the Canopy

In the high and leafy realm,
Fungi dance and critters helm,
Mossy pillows, squishy, soft,
Squirrels bouncing, aloft and oft.

A slug slides by with swagger bold,
Thinking it's a knight of old,
While pinecones drop like laughter's sound,
The humor here is all around.

The Quiet Alchemy

Rotting wood, a tasty stew,
Brings the beetles, buzzing through,
They host a ball, a banquet grand,
With stale cracker crumbs at hand.

Mushrooms bloom like party hats,
In this gourmet feast with rats,
Spinning tales of tales unsung,
While old logs serenely hum.

Embrace of the Aged

Old stones chuckle with wise grins,
As nature spruces up their sins,
Cracks give home to tiny shores,
Where ants wear crowns and hold galore.

Moss to them is vibrant hair,
They flaunt their green like debonair,
Their creaks and groans, a playful jest,
In stories told, they're never stressed.

Shades of Survival

In this patchwork quilt of green,
Creatures plot like a heist unseen,
Furry thieves with crafty schemes,
Dance between the sunlit beams.

With camouflage and sticky traps,
They twist and turn like acrobat laps,
This leafy realm, a comedy,
Where even shadows spark a spree.

The Hidden Harmonies

In the woodlands' shadowy nook,
Mossy creatures start to crook,
Dancing in colors extreme,
With giggles that bubble and scream.

Lichens wearing coats of green,
Whisper secrets, rarely seen,
They chuckle as the trees sway,
Sharing jokes in a leafy way.

Roots of Renewal

Underneath the earth so deep,
Vines and fungi start to creep,
Sprouting tales of soil's might,
While the worms laugh in delight.

Tiny worlds beneath our feet,
Where each critter finds a seat,
With roots that twist and twirl,
They spin stories, a merry whirl.

The Caretakers of Time

Fungi hats on every head,
Telling tales of the dead,
While lichens nod and agree,
Chasing clouds with glee.

They tick and tock in silence true,
Sharing snacks from morning dew,
Planting seeds of humor bright,
Guardians of laughter's light.

A World in a Whirl

Colors swirling, shapes that blend,
In this merry twist, no end,
Lichens spin, they leap and dive,
Proving that they're quite alive.

With a giggle and a sigh,
They soar through the purple sky,
In their wacky, wild parade,
Playful games they've always made.

Breathing Green: An Ode

In a world where moss can chat,
A rumbling joke from a tiny brat.
Fungi giggle, and algae dance,
Together they form a green romance.

Each spring they throw a leafy bash,
With microbes mingling in a flash.
The rocks never knew how to jest,
But now they're hosting, feeling blessed.

Underneath a vibrant dome,
Life's little beings call it home.
They wear warm coats of verdant hue,
And laugh at clouds that float on through.

So here's to mats and fluffy friends,
Where every crack of earth transcends.
A festival of joy takes flight,
In playful shades of green delight.

The Untold Chronicles of Growth

Once upon a time, in the damp,
A grandma lichen set up camp.
She told her tales of splotchy fun,
While her grandkids danced under the sun.

A tiny slug, he stole the show,
With moves that made the daisies grow.
He wiggled left, then waggled right,
While the dandelions cheered with delight.

They hosted bashes in shaded nooks,
Where beetles brought their favorite books.
And all the moss would hum along,
To the beat of a lichen's favorite song.

At last they took a grouply bow,
The green performers of here and now.
For in this patch, so full of glee,
Every moment's rich as it can be.

Clusters of Coexistence

Two buddies formed a funky pair,
Moss is shy; lichen's flair is rare.
They throw a party on the stone,
Celebrating all the ways they've grown.

One day a snail decided to join,
Sliding in, seeking that warm coin.
Lifesaving rain drummed on the ground,
A splashy dance of joy was found.

With every raindrop, laughter sprouted,
Cheers echoed, joyous tales about it!
The pebbles giggled, moss blushed deep,
As everyone shared smiles instead of sleep.

Amidst the clusters, fun would thrive,
In every crevice, they felt alive.
From spores to slugs, all joined in,
To celebrate their joy within.

Patterns of Persistence

In crevices of stone, a party grew,
Where lichen laughed at the clouds that blew.
A perennial joke kept floating around,
As moss recalled the silliest sounds.

Each day they plotted, cheerfully wild,
A prankster's dream—like a giggling child.
The sun was a spotlight, the rain a cheer,
Each gust of wind brought a wink and a sneer.

Through seasons they painted, popping with glee,
Artistry found in each green spree.
The rocks would laugh while the trees would sway,
As life burst forward in ridiculous play.

So here they sit, moss and lichen bright,
Crafting new stories from morning to night.
In the world of small, they took the chance,
To show that even the tiny can dance.

Chronicles of the Clinging

In cracks and crevices, we play,
A patch of green, come what may.
Dancing in the summer breeze,
Whispering secrets among the trees.

Stuck on rocks, we make our way,
Curbing boredom day by day.
Throw a party on a stone,
Where we gather, never alone.

Our colorful coats, a sight to see,
Fashionistas of the mossy spree.
We soak up sun, we drink the rain,
Living large, never feeling vain.

When the world above feels rough,
We laugh it off, we're tough enough.
A clinging bunch, with flair and glee,
In the most unexpected jubilee.

Beneath the Broken

Underneath the shattered bark,
We plot and scheme till it gets dark.
With glee we cling, we twist and twirl,
In this cracked world, we jump and swirl.

Mismatched shirts, a colorful crew,
We're the spices in the forest stew.
Beneath the broken, we just thrive,
Sprouting jokes, feeling alive.

When the rain drops, we have a blast,
With rib-tickling stories from the past.
Moldy bread, a feast so fine,
Join us now, and sip the brine.

Beneath the moss, don't call the cops,
Two lichen gents, we're snacking on chops.
In this wild space, we've claimed our seat,
Turning decay into something sweet.

The Unseen Ecosystem

In the chaos of the unseen scene,
We're the zany queens and kings, so keen.
Let's host a gala, a slimy bash,
With a toast to all that grows and clashes.

A millipede steals the show, so sly,
Winking at us as he passes by.
We giggle softly, we wink too,
In our tiny world, we're the select few.

It's a carnival in our humble spread,
Underneath the nasty, there's joy instead.
We cheer for spores that take a trip,
Riding the breeze on a mushroom ship.

Our shenanigans go unobserved,
In this life of laughs, we're unperturbed.
To the rhythm of nature, we softly sway,
In the unseen, we frolic and play.

Texture of Tenderness

In the soft embrace of mossy threads,
We curl up snug in our leafy beds.
With fibers dancing, all around,
Life's a squish, no crushing bound.

A tickle here, a poke over there,
With fuzzy hugs, we banter and dare.
Creating art on stones so bare,
With our gentle spots, we truly care.

Patchwork quilt of colors bright,
As we bask in the morning light.
Whispered giggles float on air,
We share our tales without a care.

In the grand tapestry of the damp,
We spin our yarns, like a forest lamp.
With texture so rich, a tactile jest,
In our cozy patch, we feel the best.

Symphony in Softness

In the damp and quiet night,
Moss plays a tune, oh what a sight!
Frogs tap dance, the leaves sway,
Nature's stage, let's all play!

With tiny hats made of dew,
The slugs slide by, they're fashion too!
A beetle's grin, a waltz in sync,
All in a world where we might sink!

The ants march on, a silly parade,
While mushrooms chuckle in the shade.
Curling roots, they laugh with ease,
Making jokes with the playful breeze!

A symphony of gooey cheer,
Where each little critter draws near.
In this realm of squishy delight,
Let's groove all day and night!

The Cradle of Colors

A patchwork quilt, so wild and bright,
In the woods, a jolly sight!
Green and gold, with splotches of red,
Where a snail sings softly to the bed.

Fungi pop like confetti in glee,
Wiggly worms throw a jubilee!
A squirrel darts in a dance of play,
Flipping leaves, oh what a display!

Tiny flowers whisper secrets bold,
To the buzzing bees, their stories told.
Each color fights for the sunlight's kiss,
In this carousel of nature's bliss!

The rocks chuckle, the soil smiles wide,
Life's a party, come join the ride!
In the cradle, where colors bloom,
Laughter echoes, dispelling the gloom!

Ethereal Echoes

In a land where whispers twirl,
Mossy carpets begin to swirl.
A tree trunk hums, a gentle tune,
Croaking frogs join in, a funny croon!

The sunlight dips like a playful sprite,
Lighting up the colors bright.
Pinecones chuckle, swinging low,
While a chipmunk joins the show!

An unseen breeze tosses leaves in jest,
While busy ants never get a rest.
With a tickle of dew on a mushroom hat,
Nature giggles, imagine that!

Ethereal echoes bounce and glide,
Chasing shadows, oh what a ride!
In these woods where humor sings,
Magic sprouts in small, silly things!

Nature's Tapestry Unfolded

A blanket woven with tales sweet,
Where caterpillars tap their feet.
On this canvas of earthy hues,
We find the laughter, we find the clues!

Dandelions wink, their seeds take flight,
Puffball clouds in a sky so bright.
A raccoon's grin, just can't be beat,
Nature's jesters, oh what a treat!

The soil chuckles with every squish,
While spiders spin an artful wish.
In this tapestry, colors collide,
Where silliness and joy abide!

As mushrooms dance in the twilight glow,
Each stitch of laughter begins to grow.
Nature's quilt, quirky and bold,
A story of fun, forever retold!

Echoes of the Enchanted

In shadows cast by fungi's cheer,
A party's brewing, lend me your ear.
The beetles dance in their tiny suits,
While slugs wear crowns made of mushroom hoots.

The ants bring snacks, all piled so high,
With crumbs of bread from a nearby pie.
The moss gives a cheer, 'Go on, eat and play!'
While snails move slow, but they're here to stay.

The Mossy Memoirs

In a world of green with secrets to share,
Where critters gossip without a care.
A worm winks slyly, with a wink and a grin,
'It's fine dining here, grab a shellfish kin!'

The lichen lounges in the morning sun,
Every drop of dew is pure fun begun.
While fuzzy mushrooms play hide and seek,
Underneath ferns, they laugh and peek.

Laments of the Lush

Oh, my dear fern, it's such a plight,
Your dress of green doesn't fit just right.
The dandelions tease with a puff and a frolic,
While you stand sulking, quite melancholic.

The mushrooms complain, 'We're misunderstood!'
'We never signed up for this neighborhood.'
In a council of greens, they'll hold a debate,
'Let's make laughter our ultimate fate!'

An Ode to the Obscure

Oh mystical moss, your charm I see,
You wiggle and giggle under the tree.
With each gentle breeze, a new tale unfolds,
Of beetles enrolled in life's wild mold.

'Come join the ruckus!' a mushroom declares,
While lichens play chess in their tiny chairs.
In this secret realm, humor prevails,
The dance of the critters tells wondrous tales.

Beneath the Bark

In a world where fungi wear a coat,
Lichens dance and make a note.
They giggle as the raindrops fall,
Sipping tea from mossy hall.

A snail winks and shuffles near,
"Who's the boss?" he quips with cheer.
They chuckle over decomposed remains,
While trade secrets hide in earthy lanes.

With every breeze, they sway and twist,
In a green parade, they can't resist.
The bugs all join this silly show,
As shadows whisper where they go.

Underneath the bark, they throw a bash,
With tiny hats and a grand ol' splash.
In this realm of spores and zest,
Who knew that fungus could jest the best?

Threads of Resilience

On rooftops high, the truth reveals,
Lichens prosper, spinning frills.
They knit a quilt from sun and air,
Thread by thread, without a care.

"Look at me!" a fiber shouts,
Clinging snugly, no room for doubts.
While weather changes, they only grin,
Unbothered by the world's din.

A drizzle falls, a dull old rain,
Yet here they laugh, ignoring pain.
They welcome clouds with open glee,
In this cozy tapestry.

Oh, the antics on a stone so cold,
Where stories of survival unfold.
Quite the mischief, these threads of delight,
Textured tough, yet ever so light.

Green Veils of Existence

A veil of green on rock and tree,
Whispers secrets, wild and free.
They swing and sway in gentle breeze,
Dancing freely among the leaves.

A beetle joins with a tap and spin,
"What's your secret, dear green kin?"
They chuckle back, with lichen glee,
"Just a touch of sun and a splash of spree!"

When winter comes, they huddle tight,
Playing cards through frosty night.
With friends they toast to mossy cheer,
Jokes and laughter fill the sphere.

In shadows cast by lofty bough,
The lichen's laughter makes us vow,
To find the humor, soft and true,
In nature's cloak of vibrant hue.

Stories in the Shadows

In cracks of stone, where suns don't peek,
Lichens gather, giggling, cheek to cheek.
With gnarled tales of bugs and dew,
Whispered secrets in the view.

By moonlight's grace, they share a jest,
"Who's the slipperiest?" is their quest.
Holding court in a twilight nook,
Each myth spun like an old, good book.

"Last week's storm? Oh, what a sight!
Did you see the snail's flight?"
In every crack and crevice bare,
Their stories flutter in the air.

In shadows cast, behold their jest,
Where life and laughter intertwine best.
From ancient roots to playful quirks,
These tiny jesters bring the works!

Underneath the Surface

Beneath the stone, a party brews,
Tiny critters in fragrant hues.
They dance on moss, a slippery floor,
While shouting, "Who invited the spore?"

The sun peeks in, a friendly glare,
A beetle waltzes without a care.
With laughter loud, they tickle the air,
A wild soirée held down there!

The sunbaked rocks in the shade blend,
Hosting meetings like they pretend.
Everyone claims a kingdom vast,
Yet all are lost in the fun, unsurpassed!

So take a look at the world below,
Where the antics of mossy mates do flow.
In this hidden realm of glee and jest,
You'll find the weirdest social fest!

Mysterious Mergers

Two fungi met on a rainy day,
With a wink, they danced in a clumsy ballet.
"Let's join forces and make it grand!"
Thus, they formed the oddest band.

"Unite our flavors!" one spored with glee,
"A soup or a stew, can't you see?"
But their blend, oh what a sight to taste,
A concoction that no chef could waste!

Pine needles joined the merry mix,
With a dash of moss for that earthy fix.
What started as strange, became quite the dish,
A recipe only the brave would wish!

So when you find things merged and mashed,
Remember their joy, not just a splash.
In quirky unions, laughter we'll find,
Where oddball friendships unwind!

An Ode to Overgrowth

Oh, how happily the green does sprawl,
In corners where sunlight dares not call.
They giggle as they climb the stone,
A vibrant crowd, never alone!

Thyme threw a rave on a sunny eve,
While clover spun tales no one could believe.
A thistle chimed in, the spikiest friend,
"In this jungle of chaos, we never end!"

A snail serenades, in lazy grooves,
As ants do the conga, each with their moves.
They toast with dewdrops, a sippin' spree,
In their tangled kingdom, wild and free!

So let us celebrate this organic spree,
Where nature's trims make a grand jubilee.
In the frolic of greens, there's too much to see,
Join the revelry—just don't make me flee!

Hushed Hues of Harmony

In silence, they gather, a colorful crew,
Whispering secrets in shades of dew.
A quiet bouquet singing tunes,
Under the gaze of lazy moons.

The mushrooms exchange their stories of old,
While ferns share giggles, brave and bold.
A truce with the grasses, all dog-eared,
Parties in shadows, forgotten and cheered.

Hues of humor spread wide like a sheet,
Where roots strum rhythm with each heartbeat.
In the still, there's a joke in the calm,
Nature's punchline—a laugh, a balm!

So slink into whispers and out of the light,
Where the colors conspire to frolic at night.
In hushed hues, a harmony plays,
A silent comedy in a myriad of ways!

The Softest Embrace

On stone they nuzzle, snug and tight,
A fashion choice, a fuzzy sight.
They've made a home, with no rent fee,
A green brigade of algae glee.

When raindrops fall, they dance and sway,
A tiny party, come what may.
They giggle soft, they tickle too,
Who knew a patch could laugh like you?

A sunny day? They wave hello,
But in the shade, they steal the show.
In every crack, they make a claim,
These little jokers, never tame.

So if you spy them, don't be shy,
Join in their fun, let worries fly.
For in their world, the small's a joy,
A lichen village, oh so coy.

Fragments of the Forgotten

Amidst the moss, they gather round,
In whispers soft, they share the sound.
Of tales once tall, now shrunk to bits,
A saga spun of fungal hits.

Underneath the ancient tree,
They plot and scheme, oh what a spree!
Where no one sees, they build their lore,
Histories told, but never bore.

With every squish and every squabble,
A merry cheer they form a wobble.
In cryptic code, they mail their notes,
Invisible ink on weathered coats.

So tread with care on crusty ground,
For who knows what merry scenes abound?
Fragments lost and stories grand,
In decayed corners, a lichen band.

Nature's Hidden Heralds

They pop up here, they pop up there,
In colors bright, with flair to spare.
Like tiny flags on nature's stage,
They whisper secrets, page by page.

On ancient rocks, they boldly stand,
A comedy troupe, both cute and grand.
They wave their arms, oh so absurd,
A crowd of cheer, without a word.

Collaborative, they break the norm,
In close-knit groups, they weather storms.
A raucous laughter fills the air,
Who knew a patch could form a flair?

So keep your eyes peeled as you roam,
These heralds tiny call the wild home.
With quirky winks, they spread delight,
A joyful patch, a carbon bite.

Growth in the Gloom

In shadows deep, they find their cheer,
Among the gloom, they persevere.
A fuzzy crew with guts so bold,
These stealthy sprouts are never told.

When sunlight fades, they thrive and feast,\nThe perfect hosts for every beast.
A banquet laid on craggy stone,
What wacky guests call it their own?

Their colors clash like socks misplaced,
A misfit squad in nature's haste.
Yet with each sigh, each little grow,
They bring forth joy, a secret show.

So hush your thoughts and take a peek,
For in the dark, their laughter's sleek.
Growth in gloom, a tale so bright,
Who knew the dark could spark delight?

Whispers of the Evergreen

In the forest, things do grin,
Mossy jokes among the kin.
Fungi giggle, roots dance low,
Nature's punchlines steal the show.

Squirrels chatter high above,
While ferns waltz, a twist of love.
Beneath the boughs, secrets share,
Laughter rustles in the air.

Tiny critters tap their feet,
On a stage where shadows meet.
Bunny hops and teases too,
As the saplings join the crew.

For in the woods, all are friends,
With humor that never ends.
Every leaf has a tale to weave,
In this quirky, green reprieve.

Shadows of Serenity

Under boughs, a banter flies,
Mushrooms throw their fits and sighs.
A cheeky beetle rolls around,
Making jokes without a sound.

Ladybugs in hats parade,
As if the sun read a charade.
In twilight hues, the laughter stings,
For who knew wings could have such flings?

Worms play poker underground,
While slugs survey their slimy ground.
A dance-off starts on shady trails,
Where silence cracked with silly tales.

Nature's jesters, never shy,
With every shade, they laugh and pry.
In the shadows where joy starts,
A wild symphony of heart and parts.

Embraces of the Earth

Roots entwined in a playful ball,
Whispering secrets, they heed the call.
Grassy trolls with goofy grins,
Tickle the soil, where the fun begins.

Caterpillars strut in style,
In their coats, they glide and smile.
The breeze plays tricks, a gentle tease,
Rustling leaves with such ease.

Mushrooms play hide-and-seek,
Underneath the trees so sleek.
The ground chuckles as they peek,
In this world where silence is unique.

Playful sprites in the muddy pools,
Splash around, they break the rules.
Joyful chaos, underfoot,
In every nook, glee's absolute.

Beneath the Blanket of Green

In emerald coats, the critters nest,
Crickets argue on who's the best.
A dance of ants in a silly march,
As mushrooms stand for a winning arch.

The sunbeams wink from above,
While rabbits nibble on what they love.
Trees whisper puns to the breeze,
As if the world is meant to tease.

Snails in line, a slow parade,
In the dim light where shadows fade.
Tickled by dew, they glide and slide,
In this funny green-glow tide.

Nature's circus, vibrant and wise,
With each chuckle, a treasure lies.
Under the blanket of kelly sheen,
The earth teems with a joy so green.

Cradle of Softness

In a cradle of green, they wiggle and squirm,
Tiny critters roam, without worry or concern.
Mossy beds they make, soft as a dream,
Living in harmony, a whimsical team.

With a chuckle and giggle, they squish and they play,
Taking their time, in a lazy ballet.
In a world so damp, they'll dance and they'll twirl,
A soggy, silly, spongy swirl!

Under the shade of a towering tree,
Dapper fungi in suits, sipping ginger tea.
Voices so merry, they share a good joke,
In a patch of delight, well, let's have a poke!

So let's all embrace their squishy delight,
These creatures of fun, thriving out of sight.
With a nudge and a wink, let the laughter flow,
In this pocket of softness, where silliness glows!

Secrets of the Soggy Ground

In the hidden depths where the dampness stays,
Whispers of secrets weave through the haze.
Wiggly worms gossip, oh what a sight,
While the raindrops chuckle and dance with delight.

With pockets of puddles, they splash about,
Sharing silly stories, without any doubt.
Fungi wear hats, like a marvelous show,
On the muddy stage, where the bold breezes blow.

Under the earth, where the mischief abounds,
Creatures concoct their most curious sounds.
Giggling grubs wiggle, as laughter ignites,
In the soggy realm, a party invites.

So let's tiptoe softly, and join the parade,
In the secrets of mud, fun is displayed.
With a wink and a grin, in this gooey domain,
We'll dance with the soggy, and sing in the rain!

Mosaic of Microcosms

In a patchwork world of squishy delight,
Microcosms thrive, from morning to night.
With colors so vibrant, oh what a scene,
Every inch a treasure, so lush and so green.

The minuscule critters host a grand fête,
With a twirl of their tails, they celebrate fate.
Each little speck, with a story to share,
In this tiny kingdom, no worry, no care.

The ants wear their shades, enjoying the breeze,
While slugs slide by, doing as they please.
With fungus and moss, at the center of cheer,
Nature's comedy show, brings smiles ear to ear.

So when you look close, through the lens of surprise,
You'll see all the laughter that bubbles and flies.
For in every small crevice, the fun never stops,
In the mosaic of life, where the joy always pops!

The Dance of Dampness

In the rhythm of pots of puddly bliss,
A grand old party that no one can miss.
With toadstools a-twirl in their polka-dot shoes,
They shimmy and shake to the dampness's blues.

Slugs in a conga, they slide with such grace,
While beetles all boogie, keeping up the pace.
In the shimmer of dew, they flounce and they hop,
Celebrating the puddles that promise won't stop.

A cha-cha of critters in droplet attire,
Bouncing and bouncing, never to tire.
Mirth in the muck, every twirl is a song,
In the dance of the damp, where the merry belong.

So join in the fun, let your laughter burst,
In the silliness found, quench your joyful thirst.
For in every soft step, take a chance to prance,
In the grand dance of dampness, let's all take a chance!

Mossy Whispers of Existence

In the damp and the green, we play hide and seek,
Mossy hats on our heads, no time to be bleak.
We dance in the shade, with a squishy delight,
While snails try to join, with all of their might.

Crispy leaves are our like cushions so grand,
We roll and we tumble, like babies we stand.
With every small breeze, we wiggle and sway,
Laughing at raindrops that fall in our play.

Oh, to be fuzzy, so cozy, and free,
On tree bark or stones, come join the spree!
Our jokes are quite punny, just listen, you'll see,
We'll tickle your heart, and as happy as we.

So here in the shades, please leave your distress,
We've pillows of moss, come take off that dress!
Let's feast on the humor, beneath skies of gray,
Life's a mossy joke, come laugh it away!

Beneath the Green Canopy

Underneath branches where sunlight won't peek,
Fungus and friends have their own little streak.
They giggle and gawk at the world passing by,
While ants trade their gossip, and slugs snicker high.

In shadows they gather, knitting stories so strange,
Where drips from the leaves become mishaps of change.
Grass blades are jesters, with moves so absurd,
They hop around laughing, not saying a word.

Oh, how they ponder, as rain starts to fall,
Do puddles hold parties? Let's throw one for all!
With mushrooms as seats, and ferns waving back,
We'll toast to the weather, in our leafy shack.

And when the sun shines, they take off their hats,
Docile they roam, while nature just chats.
Beneath the green canopy, fun never stray,
We're the lords of the laughter, so come out and play!

Fragments of Forgotten Simplicity

In cracks of old sidewalks, we gather and scheme,
Mossy thrones made of crumbs, it's a lichenous dream.
With snickers and snorts, we craft a grand jest,
Who knew that a crumb held the very best quest?

We reminisce tales of the syrupy rain,
With puddles of giggles, that wash off the pain.
A beetle still grumbles, 'Why can't I be fast?'
While we wink at the snail, that's always outclassed.

Among the wild weeds, such fragility thrives,
Laughter erupts where simplicity dives.
We shuffle and hop, in the dance of the breeze,
Wondrously messy, as we roll with ease.

So here we remain, with our earthy delight,
Crafting our humor in days and in night.
Fragments of silliness, hugged by the ground,
In every small corner, let joy be found!

Silent Growth in the Shadows

In the hush of the dusk, in a patch that feels right,
Moss stitches its secrets, so quiet, so tight.
With a whisper of green and a plop of delight,
We tickle the night, until morning's first light.

There's a fungus named Frank, who thinks he's a star,
Draping his glory from the top of a jar.
While beetles applaud and the spiders just sigh,
As wiggly worms join, to give a cheer cry.

Oh, shadows can giggle when no one's around,
With tales of sweet mischief, and joy that confounds.
We're growing by stealth, in a world full of glee,
With the silliness rolling, as wild as can be.

So come find our party, it's quiet but grand,
In the silent of leaves, come and lend us a hand.
Silent growth in the shadows, we flourish and play,
As laughter and green weave a bright, lively way!

Totality in the Tiny

In a world so small, I find a zoo,
Fungi and algae, dancing like two.
They throw a party, not a care in sight,
While I'm just watching, sipping my Sprite.

Beneath each stone, there's laughter and cheer,
A lichen convention, come gather near!
They share their secrets, whispers so sly,
As I pull out my camera, they start to deny.

With a dash of green and a sprinkle of gray,
These tiny folks know how to play.
They wiggle and jiggle, just look at them go,
Life's a party, and they steal the show!

So next time you stumble on a rock or a tree,
Remember the fun that you can't always see.
In the grandest of worlds, where wonders reside,
Tiny jesters are laughing, come take a ride!

The Spirit Beneath the Surface

Underneath the bark, there's a bustling crew,
They throw a rave, oh, if only you knew!
With confetti of spores and a glitter of dust,
These tiny wiseguys are just full of lust.

"Step right up!" they call, with a wink and a grin,
"For the greatest show, come join in our din!"
They juggle their cells, do acrobat tricks,
While I'm just amazed, thinking, 'What's in the mix?'

They spread their charm like a very fine bread,
Coziness found where most fear to tread.
Who needs grand stages when you've got a leaf?
Just watch the lichen turn mundane to thief!

So if you see patches of green on your way,
Remember the tomfoolery waiting to play.
For beneath all that surface, there's always confetti,
And spirits that whisper, "Hey, life's pretty petty!"

Brilliant Bonds of Being

In a symphony small, where the minuscule live,
Two partners unite, oh, what gifts they give!
Green hugs the gray, in a dance oh so sweet,
Like a couple of kids, in a love that can't beat.

With sassy remarks, and a penchant for fun,
They chat in the shadows, bask under the sun.
"Why worry," says one, "when we're all that we are?"
While the other just laughs, "Let's go raise the bar!"

From rocky retreats to the edges of wood,
These quirky companions create laughter, they could!
They share all their secrets, gossip like sisters,
Living life boldly, with poems and twisters.

So here's to the bonds that we can't often see,
Among humble patches, there's magic and glee.
In this tiny tableau, joy's nearly a given,
So let's tip our hats to the quirky, the livin'!

Stories from the Substrate

Once upon a rock, in a damp little nook,
The story begins in a very old book.
There's a lichen that waves, "Hey, come sit by me!"
With tales of the forest and its grand jubilee.

"Of days filled with sunlight and nights full of rain,
We dance through the seasons, never feeling pain.
We giggle and wiggle in the soft-mellow moss,
While thinking of all the big plants that we toss!"

They chuckle at roots that think they're so grand,
And while stems are all boasting, they quietly band.
With a wink and a nod, they shimmer and sway,
And life's little dramas, they keep at bay!

So gather 'round closely, lend me your ear,
For lichen's got stories that are simply a cheer!
In the depths of the earth, where all seems mundane,
There's a festival of voices, eternally in gain!

A Palette of Persistence

On a rock, a fussy friend,
Dances in the wind's own blend.
Colors splash, so bold and bright,
Laughing at the sun's delight.

With every rain, a joke is spun,
Growing under warmth and fun.
In the shade, they still do thrive,
Silly spots that jump and jive.

Textures join the merry crew,
Waving to the skies so blue.
A tickle on a turtle's shell,
Nature's giggles, can you tell?

Persistence, oh, what a prize!
In their quirks, the world complies.
Who knew grit could wear a grin?
In every crack, a jest begins.

Essence of the Understory

Beneath the trees, they roam so sly,
Winking at the passing sky.
Whispers hold a secret glee,
Ticklish fables, wild and free.

In shadowed nooks where giggles dwell,
They spin a tale, oh what the smell!
Of dampened leaves and little toes,
Underneath, a party grows.

Fungi peek, a silly sight,
Clowning under soft moonlight.
A mushroom dance in earthy shoes,
With every step, a funny bruise.

Here in the hush, they plot their schemes,
Crafting joy from quirk-filled dreams.
In the layers, laughter swells,
As nature shares its witty spells.

The Veil of Vitality

With a flourish, the green unfurls,
Hats of moss in charming swirls.
A leafy cap, a ghastly grin,
Join the party, let's begin!

Beneath the sun, they twirl and prance,
Making even stones do a dance.
Waving arms of vibrant hues,
The world around, they gladly choose.

Every drop of dew a trick,
Nature's jest in a sticky flick.
From tiny bugs to climbing vines,
All join in these jolly lines.

Veils of green that seldom tire,
Sparkle up the day much higher.
In the rich, delightful jest,
Vitality wears happiness best.

Silent Guardians of Growth

In quiet corners, they reside,
Guardians from the world outside.
What a mystery in their pause,
A secret pact with nature's laws.

On barren stones, they take their stand,
Whispering dreams without a brand.
With patient grace, they watch and cheer,
Finding joy in every tear.

Their tiny forms, a sight to see,
Wearing wisdom like a decree.
Capable of jest in the gloom,
Outlaws of the dreary room.

These guardians, so still, so sly,
Encourage growth with every sigh.
In their silence, life sparks giggles,
A sneaky twist, as nature wiggles.

Hope Amongst the Humid

In a damp old nook, where few would dare,
Lies a bright green patch, with plenty to share.
Fungi throw parties, on mossy, plush seats,
They dance in the shadows, to wild rhythmic beats.

The raindrops are guests, with hats made of dew,
Each leaf is a stage, for the fungus review.
They giggle like children, with pranks to unfold,
If you listen real close, their secrets are told.

An ant with a loaf, drags crumbs through the wet,
While snails sing to flowers, their voices are set.
In this tangled dance of the tiny and bold,
The hilarity grows, as each story is told.

So let's raise a toast, to the odd and the small,
Where the micro and macro share laughter with all.
For joy is the thread that weaves through each day,
In this whimsical world, come and join in the play.

Whispered Stories on Weathered Rock

On a slab of stone, the winds whisper low,
Tales of the critters, who steal quite the show.
A snail claims the throne, with a crown made of moss,
While a millipede scuttles, like he's the boss.

A well-worn old rock, with secrets to spill,
Holds meetings of creatures, with wit and with skill.
The shadows attend, and the sun winks in glee,
As laughter erupts, from the bugs' jubilee.

They barter in giggles, for favors and food,
And the lichen chimes in, keeping all in good mood.
With a hiccup of rain, the revelry soars,
They sip on the puddles and cheer for the chores.

These whispers from stone, oh how they delight,
In every soft crevice, joy takes flight.
For the tales of the humble, are richer than gold,
All shared on the rock, where wild dreams unfold.

Harmony in Hidden Corners

In a crack of the wall, where the sunlight is shy,
Lives a colony thriving, in colors so spry.
They giggle and wiggle, quite glad of their space,
Their cheerful existence, a delightful embrace.

Underneath the big leaf, a committee convenes,
To discuss all the antics of the nearby machines.
With jokes about raindrops, and wiggles inside,
The community laughs, with the wind as their guide.

They play hopscotch with shadows, take sight of the sun,
Their tiny adventures have only begun.
When a twinkle of dew refuses to fall,
They cheer for the moisture — it's great for them all!

So here in the corners, where few think to peep,
A carnival brews, hidden safe from the heap.
In this merry little world, with quirks to admire,
The fun never ends, as they dance on the wire.

A Symphony of Thorns and Tenderness

In a garden of prickles, a curious tune,
A concert of whispers, beneath a bright moon.
Thorns may be sharp, but their humor is grand,
With each little poke, they extend a warm hand.

A caterpillar wearing a hat made of fuzz,
Conducts the brave insects, with laughs full of buzz.
While beetles on maracas, shake to the beat,
And the thorns at the edges, all sway on their feet.

Oh, watch the young spider, with webs full of flair,
Knitting up laughter from the fluff in the air.
With a pluck of a string, the flowers will dance,
In this wild symphony, take a whimsical chance.

So gather around, where the thorny things play,
For humor and sweetness mix well in their way.
In this grand orchestra, life twirls and spins,
A comedy blooms, where the fun never thins.

The Quiet Kinship of Clinging

On stones we cling, a party of green,
Moss hats get soggy, but we're still seen.
We wiggle and squirm, through rain we dance,
Join us for breakfast, don't miss your chance.

In cracks we find joy, no worries inside,
We laugh at the rain, let it be our guide.
While others move fast, we take our sweet time,
Sharing a joke, oh, isn't it prime?

Our colors abound, in patches they gleam,
Sunshine and laughter, the world is a dream.
With every long breath, we whisper a tune,
Let's sway to the rhythm of bright afternoon.

So come take a seat, let the moss be our throne,
In this world of textures, you're never alone.
With lichens for friends, and stories to share,
We'll giggle together, in the cool evening air.

Evensong of the Underbrush

In the hush of twilight, where shadows convene,
We fungi unite, amidst leaves all so green.
A choir of crickets harmonize in the dusk,
Our bumpy old skin dances, we bask in the musk.

The fronds wave hello, the earth gives a cheer,
We pull silly faces, no need for fear.
A snail joins the chorus, with no sense of pace,
While ants keep on racing, a frantic rat race.

With each moonlit giggle, our fellowship grows,
In the thicket of laughter, our friendship just flows.
We share tales of travelers, bold and absurd,
In the wild little world, we're the quirkiest herd.

So trail through the thicket, under velvet skies,
Join our evening banquet, where the fun never dies.
With mushrooms and stories, let's feast and regroup,
In this whimsical haven, we gather the troop.

Shadows Paint the Sky

As twilight falls softly, the dance starts anew,
The shadows are painting in every hue.
We twirl like confetti on this verdant stage,
In our leafy cabaret, we laugh, disengage.

With whispers of secrets, we prance in delight,
Frogs croaking chuckles, a hilarious sight.
The fireflies chuckle, their glow leads the way,
It's a raucous parade at the end of the day.

The branches grow wobbly, the breeze, it declares,
That we're all just here for the fun that we share.
As raindrops tap shoes on the roof of the wood,
We throw our own party, oh, isn't it good?

So come join the merriment, hidden, yet free,
In shadows, we flourish, like proud greenery.
With each silly giggle, we capture the night,
Together we frolic, till dawn brings the light.

Textures of Time's Embrace

In the quiet of corners, we're weaving a tale,
From pebbles to patches, we flourish without fail.
With laughter like bubbles, we pop out and play,
Our moments like moss, they just gather each day.

With wrinkles and winks, we meet time's steady hum,
Exploring each texture, while feeling quite dumb.
The breeze brings forth stories of those long ago,
While we wriggle and giggle in bright verdant glow.

Oh, the tales that we hold in our leafy embrace,
With roots intertwined like a whimsical lace.
In cracks we find treasures, with laughter as glue,
Through seasons of golden, we blossom anew.

So gather, dear friend, in this vibrant domain,
In the world of the whimsical, welcome the strange.
With every soft moment, we cling and we live,
In the textures of time, it's the joy that we give.

Songs of the Silhouette

Beneath the ferns, they play and dance,
A mossy choir in their green expanse.
With swings made of twigs and hops on the ground,
They jest with the wind, without making a sound.

In the shadows, they gather, oh what a sight,
The silhouettes chuckle, glowing at night.
They argue about rain, and sun's silly tease,
While nibbling on crumbs from the branches and leaves.

A dandelion dreams of flying so high,
But trips on a stone and lets out a sigh.
With laughter they join, that whimsical crew,
In a world made of giggles and dew-kissed hue.

They tiptoe on rocks, all wobbly and spry,
Mountains of laughter mixing with the sky.
Under the moon, their footsteps light,
A party of shadows that's out for the night.

Whispers of the Wilderness

In the wettest corners where shadows do creep,
Mossy cabarets hold secrets to keep.
With toadstool umbrellas and whispers so sly,
They poke fun at the owls who blink with one eye.

A snail with a top hat slides over the sun,
While critters debate who's the fastest to run.
In this riot of green, the laughter's sincere,
They cheer for the days when the rain disappears.

They tickle the branches, so tickly, so neat,
As ants share their tales of their trickiest feats.
Glowing fungi giggle, contagious with glee,
In this wild, wacky world, we all want to be.

The rivers join in with a burble and splash,
While playful raccoons organize a mad dash.
Amidst tangled roots and a jolly old tree,
A festival brews, oh what joy to be free!

Guardians of Grime

Deep in the drudgery where the muck concedes,
A council of creatures shares wisdom and seeds.
The guardians grin with their grime-streaked flair,
Keeping watch o'er the underbrush, unaware.

A cabbage bug dons a crown made of dust,
As beetles debate who can run for the bus.
With squishy old socks and a party of flies,
They whisper sweet nonsense beneath cloudy skies.

Earthworms conspire beneath layers of muck,
With dreams of new homes and a bit of good luck.
They giggle in squiggles, slithering by,
As leaves do their pirouettes, reaching for the sky.

So join in the chorus of grunge and of grit,
For laughter is plentiful where the critters sit.
In a kingdom of smudges, tales sparkle and shine,
The guardians rejoice, forever entwined.

The Language of Layers

In a world full of layers, from top to below,
There's chatter and laughter where tiny folks grow.
Under blankets of leaves, a symphony croaks,
While mushrooms share gossip with a flick of their cloaks.

A snail sings a ballad, quite slow and melodious,
While roots play the bass line, cavernous and glorious.
The damp earth prattles in a grand old encore,
As lichens drop jokes like confetti on the floor.

Fleas throw a party, inviting the grime,
While critters come dancing, all perfect in time.
Underneath twinkling stars, the layers conflate,
In this muddled millennium, we all celebrate!

So gather your giggles and sprout with delight,
The language is silly, swirling through the night.
In the rhythms of nature, vibrant and spry,
With layers of laughter that float up to the sky.

Beneath the Veil of Mist

In shadows thick, we creep and crawl,
A carpet soft, yet we stand tall.
With every breeze, we wiggle free,
What a life, just wait and see!

We whisper tales to mossy friends,
Of snails and bugs—our silly trends.
Underneath the fog's embrace,
We throw our own green leafy chase!

Each drop of dew, like diamonds bright,
We sparkle through the day and night.
In secret places, we reside,
Lurking where the grasses hide!

So if you find a lichen neat,
Just chuckle at our hidden feat.
For in our world of giggles bold,
We're the jesters, green and gold!

Guardians of the Forgotten

On ancient stones, we stake our claim,
Guarding secrets, playing the game.
With tiny hats and fuzzy coats,
Who knew we'd be the kings of gloats?

Our history's written in shades of green,
In the nooks of cracks, we reign supreme.
Huddled in corners, we share our lore,
Who knew rocks could be such a chore?

We've seen the rain and felt the sun,
With whimsical tales our days are spun.
So if you wander and feel a breeze,
It's just us laughing with the trees!

We dance atop the stones so gray,
With joy unbounded, come what may.
Just tip your hat to this quirky crew,
For we're the guardians, through and through!

Nature's Forgotten Artists

We paint the rocks in colors bold,
With brushstrokes quiet, stories told.
In brilliance green, we wield our flair,
Creating murals with utmost care!

While others sprout and reach for skies,
We're the ones who quietly rise.
With patience long, we thrive in place,
Nature's artists — no rush, no race!

Our pigments mix with rain so fine,
A canvas formed of dirt and vine.
So here we sit, with hearts so light,
A whimsical gallery, pure delight!

If you should chance to stop and stare,
Just know you're caught in art's sweet snare.
For in our world, where colors gleam,
We're the dreamers of a green-filled dream!

The Balance of Fragility

We're tiny patches on surfaces wise,
With touch so soft, we mesmerize.
On bark and stone, we cling so tight,
A comedy in the morning light!

Balancing on the edge of life,
With whispers soft, we avoid the strife.
Yet here we thrive on a weathered fate,
Taking our time, we're never late!

In gentle sways, we dance along,
To nature's soft and silly song.
A fragile world that laughs and bends,
The harmony of laughter with friends!

So if you step on a patch so small,
Know it's us just having a ball.
For in this fragile balance we find,
A joyful beat, uniquely designed!

Emissaries of Endurance

In the damp of the forest, we thrive and we cling,
Munching on moss like it's the best thing.
A rock's our best friend, our steady abode,
While the world rushes by, we take it slow mode.

With patience we grow, in colors so bright,
A fungus or two join our whimsical plight.
While others rush by, with their busy routines,
We laugh at their hustle, like well-balanced queens.

A sneeze might occur, oh no! Watch us dance,
In clouds of confusion, who knew we had chance?
We drift with the wind, carefree and absurd,
An adventure awaits, if only they heard!

So here's to endurance, in patches we stand,
A kingdom of quirks, made by nature's hand.
If only you knew the games that we play,
In our world of green, it's a lichen buffet!

Chronicles of the Cold

In winter's tight grip, we don't seem to care,
We wear icy coats, with a frosty flair.
While snowflakes do fall, we're cozy and snug,
Like the couch potato, just a bit more smug.

The squirrels scurry by, with nuts for their stash,
While we munch on frost, in our chilly clash.
With folks bundled up tight, all shivering so bold,
We giggle with glee, in the chronicles cold.

Each flake tells a tale, a dance in the breeze,
While we bask in the freeze, with incredible ease.
Oh, how we revel, in a wintery glee,
In a world so still, it's as fun as can be!

So raise up a toast, with icicles bright,
To the frosty adventurers, enjoying the night.
No need for hot cocoa, or blankets so wide,
For we're lichen warriors, with nature as our guide!

Kissed by Kindness

A gust of warm air, oh what a sweet tease,
We're scattered like confetti, in the soft summer breeze.
A touch of the sun, our joyful delight,
We giggle and blush, all day long and night.

With droplets of dew, we glisten and shine,
Our world's a grand banquet, a feast so divine.
While others may fret, we frolic and roll,
In the embrace of the warmth, it's good for the soul.

A butterfly lands, curious on our back,
"Is this a massage? It's making me crack!"
We chortle and chuckle, as shadows we share,
In this lichen-laden laughter, we don't have a care.

Let kindness unite all those passing by,
In our patchy domain, beneath the blue sky.
So spread all that joy, with a wink and a smile,
For harmony, laughter, it travels a mile!

Carrying the Weight of Ages

Oh what a burden, we carry with glee,
Stuck to this rock, like no other could be!
While the trees whisper secrets of yesteryear,
We laugh at their tales, and sip on our beer.

Each crack in the stone, tells stories of old,
We're like wise old sages, not fearful or cold.
With patience and humor, we hang out and sway,
In this timeless charade, we're just here to play.

So watch how we flourish, in places unkempt,
While others stand still, we're the ones who leapt.
With each passing season, we flourish and thrive,
In the weight of the ages, we feel so alive!

So clap for the lichen, our history's cheer,
For decades and centuries, we'll still persevere.
With laughter as armor, and friendship as glue,
In this wacky old world, we'll discover anew!

Tapestries of Tenacity

In cracks of old pavement, they plot and they scheme,
A lumpy green army with a lopsided dream.
With every small raindrop, they throw a wild party,
Dancing on rooftops, oh isn't it hearty!

They giggle as cars pass, oblivious sight,
While basking in sunshine, what a glorious light.
Each patch tells a story, each hue a great tale,
Of battles they've fought, and of mushrooms they hail.

Chasing the wind, they twist and they turn,
Stubborn little folks, oh how brightly they burn.
Their friendships are steadfast, through storm and through drought,
In a world that moves fast, they say, "What's the rush about?"

So here's to the warriors, the bold and the brave,
Who thrive in the crevices, making their wave.
With a wink and a nudge, they will always survive,
In the tapestry woven, their humor's alive.

Ribbons of Resilience

In each little crack, there's a whimsical crew,
With sponges for hearts and a jolly view.
They hoot and they holler with each breather's sigh,
"Just hang on a minute, we're reaching the sky!"

With colors like confetti, they flourish and glow,
Painting the pavement, they're putting on a show.
"They said we're just fungus!" they giggle with glee,
"We're nature's surprise party, just wait and see!"

The winds may be wild and the weather a fright,
Yet up on the bricks, they party all night.
With every odd raindrop, it's a toss of a hat,
"Let's have a good laugh, and don't squish us flat!"

So raise a cheer loud for this motley brigade,
In their comical antics, no worries invade.
With ribbons of tenacity, they take to the stage,
In a world full of chaos, they're the quirky sage.

Brushstrokes of Being

On the canvas of concrete, they splash and they play,
With brushes of green, in their quirky ballet.
Each stroke is a giggle, a laugh as they grow,
Painting the mundane with their colorful flow.

They sway with delight on the edge of a ledge,
"Let's cling on together!" they chant from the edge.
In nonsense and laughter, they find their great groove,
A riotous waltz, always ready to move.

With texture and flavor, they merge and they mold,
Creating a tapestry both vivid and bold.
In sunlight or shadow, they shimmer and wink,
"Why worry so much? Just enjoy and just think!"

So let's tip our hats to this merry ensemble,
In their playful pursuits, they delight and they bumble.
In the gallery of nature, they claim their bright line,
With brushstrokes of joy, oh how they do shine!

Tales of the Tendrils

Oh, gather around for a tale of delight,
Of tendrils that twirl in the still of the night.
With a wiggle and squirm, they take to the air,
"Come dance with us, folks! We haven't a care!"

They dream of grand voyages on raindrop ships,
Of sliding down gutters on slippery tips.
With goofy ambitions, they reach for the stars,
"Who needs to be serious? We'll take our sweet spars!"

Like tiny green astronauts, striking a pose,
Adventurers at heart where the wild river flows.
With humor like jellybeans, sweet and absurd,
They make every moment a laughter-filled word.

So here's to the tendrils, the jolly and spry,
With each twist and turn, they give joy a try.
In a world that's so gnarly, they spin tales divine,
In whimsical glory, they forever will shine!

Weaving Wonders of the Wild

On a rock, I found a friend,
With a bearded rug to lend.
It tickles when the wind does swipe,
A funky dance, we twirl and gripe.

Colors blend, a patchwork quilt,
Nature dressed in greenish spilt.
We laugh at splashes, taste the air,
In this wild weave, no fuss, no care.

The Color of Contrasts

Green and gray, a mismatched pair,
Hanging out without a care.
Together they paint the rough and tough,
Growing strong—oh, ain't that enough!

Orange bursts from shades of brown,
It's a circus in this town.
The colors clash, but who's to tell?
In our world, it's just grand swell!

Moments in the Muck

Stuck in a puddle, just my luck,
This squishy mess, a comedic chuck.
I waddle through with glee and flair,
The mud is thick, but who would care?

Plop and squish, it's a slimy ball,
I leap and slip, and take a fall.
In this muck, I'm the silliest critter,
Life's a laugh, and it couldn't be fitter.

Notes from the Nurtured

Hear the whispers of the ground,
In soft tones, they dance around.
A mushroom giggles, do you know why?
It tickles roots as they reach for the sky.

From tiny spores and fuzzy threads,
We scribble tales on nature's beds.
Each note's a bouncy little rhyme,
Making us laugh, one leaf at a time.

Hues of Harmony

In the damp embrace of a chilly stone,
Colors whisper secrets, never alone.
A green parade marches, oh what a sight,
Dancing with raindrops, under the light.

Wearing sweaters of velvet, snug as a bug,
A snooze in the shadows, a warm little hug.
Tickling the noses of folks passing by,
Who stop for a moment, then clear their eye.

They giggle at patterns, like a painter's dream,
Each hue telling stories, silly and gleam.
Laughter erupts from the cracks in the floor,
Even the bricks join, their hearts wanting more.

Where whimsy meets nature, it's all in good fun,
A gathering party, no reason to run.
So raise up your glasses, to colors and cheer,
In the joyous realms, where moss draws us near.

Roots of Resilience

Beneath the soft soil, a party unfolds,
Roots twist and tangle, daring and bold.
They share silly secrets, in whispers of dirt,
While pushing through struggles, refusing to hurt.

With tiny leaf hats and a pinch of sass,
The underground crew knows how to amass.
They giggle and wiggle, a humorous bunch,
Trading their stories, over clumps they crunch.

A turnip joins in, with jokes full of glee,
Swaying to rhythms of sassy debris.
"Why did the sprout cross the old dusty road?
To laugh with the earthworm, lighten the load!"

So here's to the roots, both sturdy and grand,
Creating a banquet from this whimsical land.
In laughter and friendship, they anchor the ground,
In the heart of the soil, pure joy is found.

Whispers of the Moss

In patches of green, they sit and they chat,
Mossy companions, where silly meets that.
They whisper like gossipers, cheeky and light,
Spinning wild tales 'til the fall of the night.

"I once knew a rock that thought it could fly,
But landed too soft and let out a sigh."
They chuckle and snort, in the mid-morning dew,
Creating a chorus, just for the few.

A sprightly old pebble joins in with a grin,
"Let's prank all the grasses! Oh, where do we begin?"
They plan a grand jest, a true mossy affair,
With humor and giggles, spreading joy everywhere.

So here in the emerald, laughter does bloom,
In the heart of the forest, there's always room.
For whispers of joy, soft as the dawn,
In the world of the moss, our spirit goes on.

Textures of Time

On the bark of a tree, where the funny ones grow,
Textures of laughter stretch high and low.
Each wrinkle a story, each bump a delight,
Tickled by breezes that dance through the night.

A patchwork of colors, like a quilt on the ground,
Where the silly and subtle play merry around.
With each raucous chuckle, they wind and they weave,
Creating a tapestry, hard to believe.

"Did you see the old fungus, dressed to the nines?
With polka-dot spores and intricate lines?"
The giggles erupt in a joyful refrain,
To the rhythms of nature, in chorus they gain.

So celebrate textures, both rough and sublime,
In the artful design of the passing time.
For fun's in the fibers, the laughter combined,
In the fabric of nature, a treasure refined.

A Dance of Decay

In the damp and shaded spaces,
Lichens twirl in funny races.
With a laugh, they cling and sway,
Grooving slow, come what may.

They nibble rocks, a tasty treat,
In their world, it's quite the feat.
Between the moss, they play and peek,
In their green hats, they squeak and squeak.

On the bark, they spread a tale,
Life is languid, never frail.
Spirits high, they dance around,
In this kingdom, joy is found.

So next time when you stop and stare,
Remember the fun that's always there.
In every crack, a giggle grows,
A dance of humor, as nature flows.

Fables of the Forgotten

Beneath the tree where shadows dress,
Lichens tell their tales no less.
Whispered words in the autumn air,
Forgotten fables everywhere.

They craft their stories on stone and wood,
In ways that only the brave have understood.
Each layer thick, a jolly jest,
In their world, they humor the best.

One tells of a snail who danced so bold,
In the moonlight, oh, such stories told!
Chasing dreams on a leafy street,
With loops and swirls, they skip on their feet.

So when you wander, look closely, my friend,
For laughter and tales that never end.
In each shade, a chuckle might bloom,
Fables forgotten, their laughter in gloom.

Veins of Vitality

In the cracks of every wall,
Lichens thrive, and they stand tall.
With a grin, they stretch their limbs,
Bright greens and yellows, not on whims.

They tickle the air in colors bright,
With humor found in every sight.
A rock's embrace, they cozy stay,
In their laughter, they find a way.

From storms to sun, they never pout,
With cheeky smiles, they dance about.
Vitality runs through their veins,
In every droplet from the rains.

So cherish the quirks in nature's plan,
For each little patch is a funny clan.
Together they grow, so wild and free,
In the veins of life, there's comedy.

The Timeless Tangle

Twisting tales in tangled green,
Lichens weave where none have seen.
They shuffle 'round, a merry crew,
In a waltz that's oddly askew.

Imbued with antics from days of yore,
They decorate rocks, oh what a chore!
A tapestry of giggling bits,
Crafting joy from sunny wits.

Through the ages, they just stay put,
In their own world, there's no dispute.
With a squishy laugh and a soft embrace,
In time's grip, they find their place.

So let's celebrate this motley charm,
Where wackiness reigns with nature's calm.
In this timeless tangle, we should all dive,
For humor and life, they truly thrive.

www.ingramcontent.com/pod-product-compliance
Lightning Source LLC
Chambersburg PA
CBHW051630160426
43209CB00004B/591